Packerology
Trivia
Challenge

Green Bay Packers Football

Packerology Trivia Challenge

Green Bay Packers Football

Researched by Tom P. Rippey III

Tom P. Rippey III & Paul F. Wilson, Editors

Kick The Ball, Ltd

Lewis Center, Ohio

Trivia by Kick The Ball, Ltd

College Football Trivia

Alabama Crimson Tide	Auburn Tigers	Boston College Eagles	Florida Gators
Georgia Bulldogs	LSU Tigers	Miami Hurricanes	Michigan Wolverines
Nebraska Cornhuskers	Notre Dame Fighting Irish	Ohio State Buckeyes	Oklahoma Sooners
Oregon Ducks	Penn State Nittany Lions	Southern Cal Trojans	Texas Longhorns

Pro Football Trivia

Arizona Cardinals	Baltimore Ravens	Buffalo Bills	Chicago Bears
Cleveland Browns	Dallas Cowboys	Denver Broncos	Green Bay Packers
Indianapolis Colts	Kansas City Chiefs	Minnesota Vikings	New England Patriots
New Orleans Saints	New York Giants	New York Jets	Oakland Raiders
Philadelphia Eagles	Pittsburgh Steelers	San Francisco 49ers	Washington Redskins

Pro Baseball Trivia

Atlanta Braves	Baltimore Orioles	Boston Red Sox	Chicago Cubs
Chicago White Sox	Cincinnati Reds	Detroit Tigers	Houston Astros
Los Angeles Dodgers	Milwaukee Brewers	Minnesota Twins	New York Mets
New York Yankees	Philadelphia Phillies	Saint Louis Cardinals	San Francisco Giants

College Basketball Trivia

Duke Blue Devils	Georgetown Hoyas	Indiana Hoosiers	Kansas Jayhawks
Kentucky Wildcats	Maryland Terrapins	Michigan State Spartans	North Carolina Tar Heels
Syracuse Orange	UConn Huskies	UCLA Bruins	

Pro Basketball Trivia

Boston Celtics	Chicago Bulls	Detroit Pistons	Los Angeles Lakers
Utah Jazz			

Visit **www.TriviaGameBooks.com** for more details.

This book is dedicated to our families and friends for your unwavering love, support, and your understanding of our pursuit of our passions. Thank you for everything you do for us and for making our lives complete.

Packerology Trivia Challenge: Green Bay Packers Football; Second Edition 2011

Published by
Kick The Ball, Ltd
8595 Columbus Pike, Suite 197
Lewis Center, OH 43035
www.TriviaGameBooks.com

Edited by: Tom P. Rippey III & Paul F. Wilson
Copy Edited by: Ashley Thomas Memory
Designed and Formatted by: Paul F. Wilson
Researched by: Tom P. Rippey III

For information on ordering this book in bulk at reduced prices, please email us at pfwilson@triviagamebooks.com.

International Standard Book Number: 978-1-613320-008-7
Printed and Bound in the United States of America
10 9 8 7 6 5 4 3 2 1

Table of Contents

Dear Friend,

Thank you for purchasing our *Packerology Trivia Challenge* game book!

We have made every attempt to verify the accuracy of the questions and answers contained in this book. However it is still possible that from time to time an error has been made by us or our researchers. In the event you find a question or answer that is questionable or inaccurate, we ask for your understanding and thank you for bringing it to our attention so we may improve future editions of this book. Please email us at tprippey@triviagamebooks.com with those observations and comments.

Have fun playing *Packerology Trivia Challenge*!

Tom & Paul

Tom Rippey and Paul Wilson
Co-Founders, Kick The Ball, Ltd

PS – You can discover more about all of our current trivia game books by visiting www.TriviaGameBooks.com.

Book Format:

There are four quarters, each made up of fifty questions. Each quarter's questions have assigned point values. Questions are designed to get progressively more difficult as you proceed through each quarter, as well as through the book itself. Most questions are in a four-option multiple-choice format so that you will at least have a 25% chance of getting a correct answer for some of the more challenging questions.

We have even added Overtime in the event of a tie, or just in case you want to keep playing a little longer.

Game Options:

One Player -
To play on your own, simply answer each of the questions in all the quarters, and in the overtime section, if you'd like. Use the Player / Team Score Sheet to record your answers and the quarter Answer Keys to check your answers. Calculate each quarter's points and the total for the game at the bottom of the Player / Team Score Sheet to determine your final score.

Two or More Players –
To play with multiple players decide if you will all be competing with each other individually, or if you will form and play as teams. Each player / team will then have its own Player / Team Score Sheet to record its answer. You can use the quarter Answer Keys to check your answers and to calculate your final scores.

The Player / Team Score Sheets have been designed so that each team can answer all questions or you can divide the questions up in any combination you would prefer. For example, you may want to alternate questions if two players are playing or answer every third question for three players, etc. In any case, simply record your response to your questions in the corresponding quarter and question number on the Player / Team Score Sheet.

A winner will be determined by multiplying the total number of correct answers for each quarter by the point value per quarter, then adding together the final total for all quarters combined. Play the game again and again by alternating the questions that your team is assigned so that you will answer a different set of questions each time you play.

You Create the Game -
There are countless other ways of using *Packerology Trivia Challenge* questions. It is limited only to your imagination. Examples might be using them at your tailgate or other professional football related party. Players / Teams who answer questions incorrectly may have to perform a required action, or winners may receive special prizes. Let us know what other games you come up with!

Have fun!

Packerology Trivia Challenge

1) What was the name of the company that first sponsored Green Bay?

Answers begin on page 17

    A) Acme Packing
    B) Indian Packing
    C) Wisconsin Packers
    D) Northern Meat Packing

2) What are the Packers' official colors?

    A) Blue and White
    B) Green and White
    C) Orange and Yellow
    D) Green and Yellow

3) Green Bay's stadium has a seating capacity of over 75,000.

    A) True
    B) False

4) What year did Green Bay play its first-ever game?

    A) 1910
    B) 1915
    C) 1919
    D) 1924

5) What was Earl Lambeau's nickname?

- A) Pounder
- B) Curly
- C) Mr. Football
- D) Slick Lightning

6) In which division does Green Bay play?

- A) North
- B) East
- C) South
- D) West

7) What is the name of Green Bay's team song?

- A) "Victory March"
- B) "Go! You Packers Go!"
- C) "Packer Charge"
- D) "Cold Warriors"

8) How many times did the Packers play the College All-Stars?

- A) 1
- B) 3
- C) 5
- D) 8

9) Who did the Packers draft with their one and only "Bonus Choice" pick?

    A) Al Carmichael
    B) Don Hutson
    C) Paul Hornung
    D) Bart Starr

10) In which Super Bowl was the NFL Champion first awarded a Vince Lombardi Trophy?

    A) IV
    B) V
    C) VII
    D) X

11) Who was the last Packer head coach to win NFL Coach of the Year?

    A) Vince Lombardi
    B) Mike Holmgren
    C) Mike McCarthy
    D) Lindy Infante

12) The Cowboys have never beaten Green Bay at Lambeau Field.

    A) True
    B) False

13) What is the nickname of Lambeau Field?

  A) Greenland
  B) Ice Pond
  C) Victory Field
  D) Frozen Tundra

14) Who was the first player to do the "Lambeau Leap"?

  A) Ahman Green
  B) Sterling Sharpe
  C) LeRoy Butler
  D) James Lofton

15) What year did Lambeau Field open?

  A) 1939
  B) 1944
  C) 1951
  D) 1957

16) When was the last year Green Bay did not play a Monday Night Football game?

  A) 1992
  B) 1995
  C) 1999
  D) 2003

17) What position did Mike McCarthy play in college?

    A)   Offensive lineman
    B)   Tight end
    C)   Linebacker
    D)   Quarterback

18) From which college has Green Bay drafted the most players?

    A)   Notre Dame
    B)   Wisconsin
    C)   Alabama
    D)   Minnesota

19) Who holds the Green Bay career rushing record?

    A)   Jim Taylor
    B)   Ahman Green
    C)   Dorsey Levins
    D)   John Brockington

20) How many weeks were Packer players named NFL Rookie of the Week in 2010?

    A)   0
    B)   1
    C)   3
    D)   5

21) Did Brett Favre win his first game as a starter for the Packers?

   A) Yes
   B) No

22) How do Green Bay players generally travel to the stadium during training camp?

   A)   Ride a team bus
   B)   Walk
   C)   Ride a bike
   D)   Take a plane

23) Which Green Bay head coach has the most wins?

   A)   Mike Holmgren
   B)   Vince Lombardi
   C)   Curly Lambeau
   D)   Mike Sherman

24) What year did Green Bay first offer a stock sale?

   A)   1919
   B)   1923
   C)   1928
   D)   1936

25) Who holds the Green Bay record for passing yards in a single game?

    A) Lynn Dickey
    B) Brett Favre
    C) Don Horn
    D) Tobin Rote

26) Which city would host an occasional Packer home game until 1995?

    A) Sheboygan
    B) Minneapolis
    C) Madison
    D) Milwaukee

27) How many times has Green Bay played in the Super Bowl?

    A) 2
    B) 4
    C) 5
    D) 7

28) What year did the "G" logo first appear on the Packer helmet?

    A) 1950
    B) 1956
    C) 1961
    D) 1967

29) Have the Packers ever played the Bears in the playoffs?

   A) Yes
   B) No

30) Who is the only player to have gained more than 2,000 total yards for the Packers in one season?

   A) Ahman Green
   B) Sterling Sharpe
   C) Dorsey Levins
   D) John Brockington

31) Who led the Packers in sacks during the 2010 regular season?

   A) A.J. Hawk
   B) Cullen Jenkins
   C) Clay Matthews
   D) B.J. Raji

32) Which team has Green Bay played more often than any other in postseason games?

   A) Pittsburgh Steelers
   B) San Francisco 49ers
   C) Detroit Lions
   D) Dallas Cowboys

33) What are the most regular season wins the Packers have had in a single season?

    A) 10
    B) 12
    C) 13
    D) 15

34) Which Packer holds the record for points scored in a single quarter?

    A) Don Hutson
    B) Jim Taylor
    C) John Brockington
    D) Sterling Sharpe

35) How many defensive touchdowns did the Packers have in the 2010 regular season?

    A) 1
    B) 3
    C) 4
    D) 6

36) What single season NFL record did the Packers set in 1983?

    A) Fewest total yards allowed
    B) Most sacks
    C) Fewest passing attempts
    D) Most overtime games

37) Who is the play-by-play announcer for the Packers Radio Network?

    A) Wayne Larrivee
    B) Larry McCarren
    C) Kevin Harlan
    D) Ross Scheiderman

38) Aaron Rodgers had a better completion percentage in the 2010 regular season than Matt Flynn.

    A) True
    B) False

39) In the lyrics of the Green Bay team song, what colors are mentioned?

    A) Gold and Green
    B) Blue and Gold
    C) Green and Yellow
    D) Black and Blue

40) What does the sign over the field entrance of the Packers' locker room say?

    A) Win like champions
    B) Victory is found within
    C) Winning is a habit
    D) Leave no regrets on the field

41) How many teams have never beaten the Packers at Lambeau Field?

    A) 1
    B) 3
    C) 5
    D) 7

42) Who holds the Green Bay record for receiving yards in a season?

    A)   James Lofton
    B)   Sterling Sharpe
    C)   Robert Brooks
    D)   Donald Driver

43) What year was the infamous "Ice Bowl" between Green Bay and the Dallas Cowboys?

    A)   1967
    B)   1972
    C)   1977
    D)   1983

44) How many NFL Championships has Green Bay won?

    A)   10
    B)   13
    C)   15
    D)   17

45) Which Packer holds the team's single game rushing record?

   A) Najeh Davenport
   B) Jim Taylor
   C) Ahman Green
   D) Billy Grimes

46) Who was the last Packer to win the Super Bowl MVP?

   A) Brett Favre
   B) Desmond Howard
   C) Bart Starr
   D) Aaron Rodgers

47) How many one-season head coaches has Green Bay officially had?

   A) 2
   B) 4
   C) 6
   D) 7

48) Did Vince Lombardi coach another NFL team after leaving the Packers?

   A) Yes
   B) No

49) Who holds the Green Bay record for points scored in a career?

    A)   Chris Jacke
    B)   Don Hutson
    C)   Paul Hornung
    D)   Ryan Longwell

50) In which year did the Packers first celebrate a victory over the Chicago Bears?

    A)   1921
    B)   1925
    C)   1932
    D)   1937

Imagine how the landscape of sports has been changed by air travel. That landscape began to take shape in 1940 when the Green Bay Packers became the first NFL team to travel to a road game by plane. The team flew in two "glamorous" DC-3s that had a cruising speed of 150 mph and a seating capacity of approximately 25 passengers. Due to the general fear of flying during those days, many players took out life insurance policies in case of a crash. Many fans showed up to see the team take off in what was considered at the time to be an enormous plane - an astonishing 64 feet long.

1) B – Indian Packing (The company gave $500 to the team to purchase uniforms and equipment.)

2) D – Green and Yellow

3) B – False (Current seating capacity is 72,928.)

4) C – 1919 (Green Bay went 10-1 with their only loss coming in the last game to the Beloit Professionals.)

5) B – Curly (Earl "Curly" Lambeau is credited with being the force behind the foundation of the Packers.)

6) A – North (Along with Chicago, Minnesota and Detroit.)

7) B – "Go! You Packers Go!" (Eric Karll composed the song in 1931. It is played at home games before the National Anthem.)

8) D – 8 (The NFL Champion played the College All-Stars for 41 years starting in 1934. The Packers went 6-2 against the All-Stars and last played in the charitable game in 1968.)

9) C – Paul Hornung (The bonus choice was essentially the No. 1 overall pick of the draft and was used by the NFL from 1947-58. The Packers won the draw in 1957 and chose Heisman winner Paul Hornung.)

10) B – V (Commissioner Pete Rozelle renamed the trophy shortly after Lombardi's death in 1970 – the same year as the merger between the AFL and NFL.)

11) D – Lindy Infante (He won this award in 1989 after leading the team to a 10-6 record and the Packers' first winning season in seven years.)

12) B – False (The Packers are 6-1 all-time in the regular season and 1-0 in the postseason against Dallas in Green Bay, with the only loss coming in 2008 [Packers 16, Cowboys 27].)

13) D – Frozen Tundra (Commonly used to reference the frigid temperatures at the stadium on game day.)

14) C – LeRoy Butler (In 1993 cornerback LeRoy Butler returned a fumble for a touchdown against the Raiders, starting one of the most recognized traditions in professional football.)

15) D – 1957 (Construction cost was $960,000. This is the oldest stadium in the NFL.)

16) A – 1992 (The Packers have played on Monday Night Football at least once every year since 1993 and have an overall record of 27-29-1.)

17) B – Tight end (McCarthy played at Baker University in Baldwin City, Kan. He was a captain and named All-Conference his senior year.)

18) D – Minnesota (41 players)

19) B – Ahman Green (8,322 yards rushing from 2000-06, 2009)

20) A – 0 (The last Packer to be named NFL Rookie of the Week was Clay Matthews in Week 10 of 2009.)

21) A – Yes (Favre led the Packers to a 17-3 victory vs. the Steelers in Week 4 of the 1992 season.)

22) C – Ride a bike (Since the days of Vince Lombardi, players generally ride the short distance to practice on a bike offered by a local kid.)

23) C – Curly Lambeau (212 wins from 1921-49)

24) B – 1923 (A rain-soaked season kept fans away in 1922 and the team almost folded from the high debt load. The team was turned into a non-profit organization and 1,000 shares were sold to local merchants in the first stock sale.)

25) A – Lynn Dickey (He completed 35 passes for 418 yards against Tampa Bay in 1980.)

26) D – Milwaukee (The Packers played annual games in Milwaukee from 1933-94.)

27) C – 5 (Super Bowls I, II, XXXI, XXXII and XLV)

28) C – 1961 (Sometimes referred to as the "Lombardi G," the Packer helmet has been relatively unchanged since the addition of the logo.)

29) A – Yes (The Packers lost 14-33 to the Bears in the 1941 Western Division Playoffs and beat the Bears 13-6 in the 2010 NFC Championship.)

30) A – Ahman Green (2,250 yards in 2003)

31) C – Clay Matthews (Matthews recorded 13.5 sacks during the regular season. Second on the team was Cullen Jenkins with 7.0 sacks.)

32) D – Dallas Cowboys (The Packers have faced both the Cowboys and New York Giants six times in the postseason. Green Bay is 2-4 all-time against the Cowboys and 4-2 against the Giants.)

33) C – 13 (The Packers won 13 games four times during the regular season [1962, 1996, 1997 and 2007].)

34) A – Don Hutson (Hutson scored 29 points [four touchdowns and five extra points] in the second quarter against Detroit on Oct. 7, 1945.)

35) C – 4 (Nick Collins returned a fumble and Clay Matthews, Charles Woodson and Desmond Bishop each returned an interception.)

36) D – Most overtime games (Green Bay played in five overtime games going 2-3. The Packers are 13-12-4 [.517] all-time in overtime games.)

37) A – Wayne Larrivee (Larrivee has been the team's play-by-play announcer since 1999.)

38) A – True (Rodgers had a 65.7 completion percentage [312-475] and Flynn completed 60.6 percent of his passes [40-66].)

39) B – Blue and Gold ("Fight on, you blue and gold....")

40) D – Leave no regrets on the field

41) B – 3 (Green Bay is undefeated at home against the Cardinals [6-0], Ravens [2-0] and Broncos [3-0].)

42) C – Robert Brooks (Brooks gained 1,497 yards in 1995.)

43) A – 1967 (The -13 degree [-46 with wind chill] temperature for this NFL Championship game is a Lambeau Field record for the coldest game. 50,000 fans braved the weather to see their Packers win a third consecutive title [21-17].)

44) B – 13 (1929-31, 1936, 1939, 1944, 1961, 1962, 1965-67, 1996 and 2010)

45) C – Ahman Green (He gained 218 yards on 20 carries against Denver on Dec. 28, 2003.)

46) D – Aaron Rodgers (Rodgers won the award in Super Bowl XLV after passing for 304 yards and three touchdowns.)

47) A – 2 (Ray McLean [1958] and Ray Rhodes [1999] Note: Ray McLean and Hugh Devore were co-head coaches for two games in 1953.)

48) A – Yes (Lombardi coached the Redskins to a 7-5-2 record in 1969, ending the franchise's streak of 14 consecutive losing seasons.)

49) D – Ryan Longwell (1,054 career points scored from 1997-05: 376 PATs and 226 FGs.)

50) B – 1925 (Green Bay beat the Bears 14-10 in the fourth meeting between the teams.)

Note: All answers valid as of the end of the 2010 season, unless otherwise indicated in the question itself.

1) For which Packer great is the Green Bay practice facility named?

Answers begin on page 37

   A)   Don Hutson
   B)   Vince Lombardi
   C)   Bart Starr
   D)   Ray Nitschke

2) What number did Bart Starr wear?

   A)   7
   B)   10
   C)   12
   D)   15

3) When was the last time the Packers drafted a running back in the first round?

   A)   1990
   B)   1994
   C)   1997
   D)   2003

4) Which decade did Green Bay have the best winning percentage?

   A)   1930s
   B)   1960s
   C)   1970s
   D)   1990s

5) Does Green Bay have an all-time winning record against Chicago?

    A) Yes
    B) No

6) What is the Green Bay record for most consecutive 10-win seasons?

    A) 3
    B) 4
    C) 6
    D) 8

7) What are the most rushing yards for the Packers in a Super Bowl?

    A) 121
    B) 145
    C) 163
    D) 209

8) Where did Curly Lambeau play college football?

    A) Notre Dame
    B) Princeton
    C) Army
    D) Ohio State

9) For which college did Packer greats Don Hutson and Bart Starr play?

    A) Wisconsin
    B) Harvard
    C) Southern Cal
    D) Alabama

10) How many teams has Green Bay played 50 or more times in the regular season?

    A) 7
    B) 9
    C) 11
    D) 13

11) What are the most points the Packers have allowed in a playoff game?

    A) 38
    B) 42
    C) 45
    D) 51

12) Against which team was Green Bay's first league win?

    A) Columbus Panhandles
    B) Minnesota Marines
    C) Chicago Staleys
    D) New York Brickley Giants

13) Did Aaron Rodgers have more than 500 passing attempts in the regular season in 2010?

   A) Yes
   B) No

14) Who was the last player to gain over 200 yards rushing in a game against Green Bay?

   A) Tiki Barber
   B) Gale Sayers
   C) Adrian Peterson
   D) Shaun Alexander

15) What is the Lambeau Field record for longest field goal kicked by a Packer?

   A) 46
   B) 49
   C) 53
   D) 58

16) Which of the following Packers never led the league in scoring?

   A) Paul Hornung
   B) Don Hutson
   C) Ryan Longwell
   D) Chester Marcol

17) Against which team did Brett Favre break the NFL career touchdown passing record?

    A) Denver Broncos
    B) Chicago Bears
    C) San Diego Chargers
    D) Minnesota Vikings

18) When was the last time the Packers had over 500 yards of total offense?

    A) 2001
    B) 2003
    C) 2005
    D) 2010

19) How many times has Green Bay had the number one overall draft pick?

    A) 2
    B) 3
    C) 5
    D) 6

20) Green Bay is Mike McCarthy's first head coaching position at any level.

    A) True
    B) False

21) How many yards is the longest rushing play in Green Bay history?

    A) 79
    B) 84
    C) 92
    D) 98

22) Which team has Green Bay never beaten at Lambeau?

    A) New York Jets
    B) Tennessee Titans
    C) Jacksonville Jaguars
    D) Buffalo Bills

23) By which college football team's stadium was Lambeau Field's design inspired?

    A) Notre Dame
    B) Michigan
    C) Wisconsin
    D) Southern Cal

24) How many times has Green Bay played in the NFC Wild Card Playoff Game?

    A) 3
    B) 5
    C) 7
    D) 10

25) The Packers have never been outgained in any Super Bowl appearance.

    A) True
    B) False

26) In which year did the Packers win their first playoff game?

    A) 1922
    B) 1926
    C) 1929
    D) 1936

27) How many times has Green Bay lost a home opener (first game played in the state of Wisconsin)?

    A) 30
    B) 35
    C) 39
    D) 42

28) Who is the only Green Bay player to be named NFL Offensive Rookie of the Year?

    A) John Brockington
    B) Brett Favre
    C) Jim Taylor
    D) Sterling Sharpe

29) How many years did Earl Lambeau play football for the Packers?

   A) 5
   B) 7
   C) 9
   D) 11

30) How many games did Green Bay play in its first NFL season?

   A) 4
   B) 6
   C) 8
   D) 9

31) What is the Green Bay record for the longest punt?

   A) 78
   B) 83
   C) 87
   D) 90

32) Do the Packers have an all-time regular season winning record against the AFC?

   A) Yes
   B) No

33) Who was the last Packer to have over 100 receptions in a single season?

    A)   Sterling Sharpe
    B)   Donald Driver
    C)   Robert Brooks
    D)   Javon Walker

34) Who is the only Green Bay player to be named NFL Defensive Rookie of the Year by the Associated Press?

    A)   AJ Hawk
    B)   Nick Barnett
    C)   Willie Buchanon
    D)   Clay Matthews

35) To which team did Green Bay suffer its worst loss in its first NFL season?

    A)   Racine Legion
    B)   Chicago Staleys
    C)   Chicago Cardinals
    D)   Hammond Pros

36) Who was Green Bay's first opponent at Lambeau Field?

    A)   Chicago Bears
    B)   Pittsburgh Steelers
    C)   Minnesota Vikings
    D)   Detroit Lions

37) For how many yards was the longest touchdown drive by the Packers in 2010 regular season?

    A) 87
    B) 91
    C) 93
    D) 97

38) Which Packer has been named First-team All-Pro the most number of years?

    A) Brett Favre
    B) Willie Wood
    C) James Lofton
    D) Forrest Gregg

39) Who holds the Green Bay record for passing yards in a season?

    A) Brett Favre
    B) Bart Starr
    C) Lynn Dickey
    D) Don Majkowski

40) Green Bay has an all-time regular season winning record against every NFL Division.

    A) True
    B) False

41) Who holds the Green Bay record for receiving yards in a single game during the regular season?

A) Don Hutson
B) Billy Howton
C) Javon Walker
D) Don Beebe

42) Who was the last quarterback to start for the Packers before Brett Favre began his consecutive-start streak?

A) Mike Tomczak
B) Blair Keil
C) Don Majkowski
D) Anthony Dilweg

43) When was the last time the Packers had a punt blocked?

A) 1998
B) 2002
C) 2005
D) 2009

44) Since 1975, how many Packers have recorded over 1,000 career tackles?

A) 2
B) 3
C) 5
D) 6

45) Did Brett Favre have more than 60,000 career passing yards as a Packer?

    A) Yes
    B) No

46) Who holds the Packer record for career sacks?

    A) Aaron Kampman
    B) Reggie White
    C) Tim Harris
    D) Kabeer Gbaja-Biamila

47) How many times have Packer receivers gained more than 1,250 yards receiving in a single season?

    A) 4
    B) 7
    C) 9
    D) 12

48) How many times have Packer head coaches been named NFL Coach of the Year by the Associated Press?

    A) 1
    B) 2
    C) 3
    D) 5

49) In how many different decades have the Packers won at least 85 regular-season games?

    A) 2
    B) 4
    C) 5
    D) 7

50) How many Green Bay players have won Super Bowl MVP?

    A) 1
    B) 2
    C) 3
    D) 5

Vince Lombardi will always stand out as one of football's most memorable and charismatic leaders. However, who would have guessed that he could twist the arm of the most powerful man in the world, the President of the United States? Due to the Berlin Crisis in 1961, Ray Nitschke, Boyd Dowler and Paul Hornung had been called to service and would not be able to participate in the 1961 NFL Championship game. Nitschke and Dowler were fortunate enough to get weekend passes but Hornung was not so lucky. So Lombardi put his powers of persuasion to work. He made a phone call to President Kennedy and they agreed that Hornung was not going to individually win the war and that fans deserved to see the two best teams play for the championship. Kennedy released Hornung from service and the Packers beat the Giants 37-0 with Hornung scoring 19 points.

1) A – Don Hutson (The Don Hutson Center indoor practice facility opened in 1994 and is located across the street from the stadium.)

2) D – 15 (Bart Starr played for the Packers from 1956-71.)

3) A – 1990 (The Packers drafted Darrell Thompson, University of Minnesota, with the 19th overall pick.)

4) B – 1960s (Green Bay went 96-37-5 for a .714 winning percentage.)

5) B – No (The Packers are 84-92-6 [.478] against Chicago.)

6) B – 4 (Green Bay went 11-5 in 1995, 13-3 in 1996, 13-3 in 1997, and 11-5 in 1998.)

7) C – 163 (Green Bay rushed the ball 41 times against the Raiders in Super Bowl II.)

8) A – Notre Dame (Lambeau played fullback for Knute Rockne and was the only freshman on the team in 1918 to letter. He was unable to play following his freshman year and returned home to Green Bay.)

9) D – Alabama (Lambeau noticed Hutson during an Alabama practice in preparation to face Stanford in the 1935 Rose Bowl. Bart Starr was selected in the 17th round of the 1956 draft.)

10) A – 7 (Bears [178], Lions [161], Vikings [99], Rams [89], Cardinals [69], 49ers [56] and Bucs [51])

11) D – 51 (The Packers lost 45-51 to the Cardinals in the 2009 NFC Wild Card Playoff.)

12) B – Minnesota Marines (The Packers beat the Marines 7-6 on Oct. 23, 1921.)

13) B – No (Rodgers completed 312 of 475 passes in 2010 for 28 touchdowns and 11 interceptions.)

14) D – Shaun Alexander (He rushed for 201 yards against the Packers in 2006.)

15) C – 53 (This has been done multiple times by multiple players, most recently by Mason Crosby in 2008.)

16) C – Ryan Longwell (His highest ranking was No. 3. Hutson led the league five times, Hornung three times and Marcol two times.)

17) D – Minnesota Vikings (Favre surpassed Marino [420 career TD passes] in Week 4 of the 2007 season and finished his career with 508 touchdown passes in the regular season [442 in Green Bay].)

18) D – 2010 (Green Bay gained 515 yards against the Giants in Week 16.)

19) A – 2 (In 1957 Green Bay drafted Paul Hornung from Notre Dame. Randy Duncan from Iowa was taken with the first pick overall in 1959.)

20) A – True (McCarthy was an offensive coordinator with the 49ers prior to joining the Packers as head coach in 2006. He had never been a head coach in college or the NFL.)

21) D – 98 (Ahman Green set this record in 2003 against the Broncos. The previous record was 97 yards set by Andy Uram in 1939.)

22) C – Jacksonville Jaguars (The Packers lost 25-28 to Jacksonville in 2004, the only time the two teams have played at Green Bay.)

23) B – Michigan (One of the original designers was a Michigan alumnus who brought the bowl design to Green Bay, which is now an exclusive characteristic of NFL stadiums.)

24) D – 10 (The Packers are 6-4 all time in wild-card playoff games [1993-95, 1998, 2001-04, and 2009-10].)

25) B – False (The Steelers outgained the Packers by 49 yards in Super Bowl XLV.)

26) D – 1936 (Green Bay beat the Redskins 21-6 in the NFL Championship.)

27) C – 39 (Since 1922, the Packers are 48-39-2 [.551] in home openers.)

28) A – John Brockington (Brockington received this award in 1971 after leading the NFC in rushing yards with 1,105 yards.)

29) D – 11 (Lambeau played halfback for the Packers from 1919-29.)

30) B – 6 (The Packers finished 3-2-1 in 1921.)

31) D – 90 (Don Chandler boomed a 90-yarder against San Francisco in 1965.)

32) B – No (Green Bay has an all-time record of 97-104-3 against the AFC for a .483 winning percentage.)

33) C – Robert Brooks (He pulled in 102 receptions for 1,494 yards and 13 touchdowns in 1995.)

34) C – Willie Buchanon (He won the award in 1972 after starting all 14 games and tying as team leader in interceptions [4] and fumble recoveries [3].)

35) B – Chicago Staleys (The Packers lost 0-20 to the team that would become the Chicago Bears in 1922.)

36) A – Chicago Bears (Green Bay won the dedication game 21-17.)

37) C – 93 (Greg Jennings capped off a 10-play drive in the second quarter against the Cowboys in Week 9 with a touchdown reception from Aaron Rodgers.)

38) D – Forrest Gregg (Gregg was named First-team All-Pro nine times [1960, 1962-67].)

39) C – Lynn Dickey (He passed for 4,458 yards in 1983.)

40) B – False (Green Bay has a losing record against the AFC East [14-30, .318] and AFC South [27-29-1, .482].)

41) B – Billy Howton (He gained 257 yards on seven receptions against the Rams in 1956.)

42) C – Don Majkowski (Majkowski started the first three games of 1992 before Favre began his consecutive start streak.)

43) D – 2009 (Tampa Bay blocked a Jeremy Kapinos punt in Week 9.)

44) B – 3 (John Anderson recorded 1,020 tackles from 1978-89, Nick Barnett recorded 1,010 from 2003-10, and Johnnie Gray recorded 1,001 from 1975-83.)

45) A – Yes (Favre ended his Green Bay career with a total of 61,655 yards.)

46) D – Kabeer Gbaja-Biamila (Kabeer passed Reggie White in 2007 to become the Packers' all-time sack leader with 74.0 career sacks. Sacks did not become an NFL statistic until 1982.)

47) D – 12 (The last player to accomplish this feat was Greg Jennings with 1,264 yards in 2010.)

48) B – 2 (Vince Lombardi [1959] and Lindy Infante [1989])

49) B – 4 (1930s [86 games], 1960s [96 games], 1990s [93 games, and 2000s [95 games])

50) C – 3 (Bart Starr [Super Bowl I and II], Desmond Howard [Super Bowl XXXI] and Aaron Rodgers [Super Bowl XLV])

Note: All answers valid as of the end of the 2010 season, unless otherwise indicated in the question itself.

1) Since 1970, how many times has Green Bay lost in the NFC Championship game?

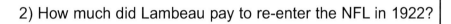

Answers begin on page 56

   A) 1
   B) 2
   C) 4
   D) 5

2) How much did Lambeau pay to re-enter the NFL in 1922?

   A) $100
   B) $250
   C) $500
   D) $675

3) Since 1922, which year was Green Bay's first 10-win season?

   A) 1929
   B) 1938
   C) 1942
   D) 1954

4) Which Packers head coach has the second most wins while at Green Bay?

   A) Mike Sherman
   B) Mike Holmgren
   C) Dan Devine
   D) Vince Lombardi

5) What is the largest margin of victory for Green Bay in a playoff game?

    A) 28
    B) 33
    C) 37
    D) 42

6) Who holds the Packer career record for receiving yards?

    A) James Lofton
    B) Don Hutson
    C) Boyd Dowler
    D) Antonio Freeman

7) Which of the following Green Bay quarterbacks never threw five touchdown passes in a single game?

    A) Don Horn
    B) Lynn Dickey
    C) Brett Favre
    D) Bart Starr

8) How many combined kickoffs and punts were returned for touchdowns by the Packers in 2010?

    A) 0
    B) 2
    C) 4
    D) 5

9) What is Green Bay's record for points after touchdown made in a single game?

    A) 5
    B) 7
    C) 8
    D) 10

10) Which is the only decade the Packers failed to have a 10-win season?

    A) 1920s
    B) 1940s
    C) 1950s
    D) 1970s

11) Every successful two-point conversion by the Packers has been a pass play.

    A) True
    B) False

12) In 2010 how many games did Aaron Rodgers pass for more than 300 yards?

    A) 2
    B) 3
    C) 5
    D) 7

13) Since 1982, how many times has a linebacker led the Packers in sacks?

   A) 3
   B) 6
   C) 8
   D) 10

14) Who is the only Packer defender to have recorded 10 interceptions in a single season?

   A) Bobby Dillon
   B) Irv Comp
   C) LeRoy Butler
   D) Charles Woodson

15) Which Packers coach has the best winning percentage?

   A) Curly Lambeau
   B) Vince Lombardi
   C) Mike McCarthy
   D) Phil Bengston

16) What is the Green Bay record for highest total offense in a single game?

   A) 562 yards
   B) 598 yards
   C) 628 yards
   D) 641 yards

17) Who was the last Green Bay player to record over 150 tackles in a single season?

    A) A.J. Hawk
    B) Nick Barnett
    C) Bernardo Harris
    D) Rich Wingo

18) What is the Packer record for most consecutive losses?

    A) 5
    B) 7
    C) 9
    D) 11

19) When was the last time the season leading passer for Green Bay had less than 1,000 yards passing?

    A) 1955
    B) 1962
    C) 1973
    D) 1981

20) Who was the last receiver to lead the Packers in scoring?

    A) James Lofton
    B) Sterling Sharpe
    C) Antonio Freeman
    D) Donald Driver

21) What is Green Bay's winning percentage at home?

    A) .541
    B) .597
    C) .622
    D) .641

22) Did the Packers ever have official cheerleaders?

    A) Yes
    B) No

23) Who was the last Packer to have his number retired?

    A) Ray Nitschke
    B) Bart Starr
    C) Don Hutson
    D) Reggie White

24) When was the only time the Packers gained over 2,500 rushing yards as a team in a single season?

    A) 1989
    B) 1995
    C) 2003
    D) 2007

25) Brett Favre had more than three times as many career pass attempts in the playoffs as Bart Starr.

A) True
B) False

26) Which was the opposing team in Green Bay's last overtime game?

A) Denver Broncos
B) Philadelphia Eagles
C) Washington Redskins
D) Miami Dolphins

27) Who is the only Green Bay kicker to have been named NFC Rookie of the Year?

A) Don Chandler
B) Chris Jacke
C) Jan Stenerud
D) Chester Marcol

28) Since 1970, how many times has a non-kicker led the Packers in scoring?

A) 3
B) 5
C) 7
D) 8

29) In which year did Green Bay get their 1,000 all-time NFL win?

    A) 1993
    B) 1996
    C) 2000
    D) 2002

30) What is the combined winning percentage for coaches who lasted only one season at Green Bay?

    A) .380
    B) .447
    C) .501
    D) .543

31) In how many regular season games did a Packer running back rush for more than 100 yards in 2010?

    A) 1
    B) 4
    C) 6
    D) 8

32) What is Green Bay's longest drought between playoff appearances since 1936?

    A) 7 years
    B) 10 years
    C) 12 years
    D) 15 years

33) Against which AFC team does Green Bay have the best all-time winning percentage (min. 3 games)?

    A)   Cleveland Browns
    B)   San Diego Chargers
    C)   Kansas City Chiefs
    D)   New England Patriots

34) How did Green Bay score its first points in Super Bowl I?

    A)   Touchdown Pass
    B)   Safety
    C)   Field Goal
    D)   Touchdown Run

35) Has Green Bay ever failed to rush for 1,000 yards as a team in a season?

    A)   Yes
    B)   No

36) In how many consecutive regular-season games did Brett Favre start while with the Packers?

    A)   237
    B)   245
    C)   255
    D)   275

37) Who was the first round pick for the Packers in the 2011 NFL Draft?

A) Davon House
B) Alexander Green
C) Randall Cobb
D) Derek Sherrod

38) Since 1932, who is the only Packer to lead the team in passing and rushing in the same year?

A) Irv Comp
B) John Hadl
C) Arnie Herber
D) Tobin Rote

39) Who scored Green Bay's winning touchdown in the "Ice Bowl"?

A) Boyd Dowler
B) Jerry Kramer
C) Bart Starr
D) Chuck Mercein

40) When was the last time the leading rusher for Green Bay gained less than 500 yards for the season?

A) 1998
B) 2001
C) 2007
D) 2010

41) When was the last time the Packers went undefeated in the preseason?

   A) 1991
   B) 1997
   C) 2000
   D) 2005

42) What is the Green Bay record for margin of victory?

   A) 42
   B) 46
   C) 50
   D) 53

43) In which state did the Packers first have spring practice?

   A) Texas
   B) Wisconsin
   C) Florida
   D) Arizona

44) Who coached Green Bay after Earl Lambeau?

   A) Vince Lombardi
   B) Gene Ronzani
   C) Lisle Blackbourn
   D) Phil Bengston

45) Who scored the first touchdown for the Packers in Super Bowl XLV?

    A) Donald Driver
    B) Nick Collins
    C) Jordy Nelson
    D) Greg Jennings

46) Did Vince Lombardi win his last game as a Packer head coach?

    A) Yes
    B) No

47) Where did the Packers play their home games before Lambeau Field?

    A) Bellevue Park
    B) County Stadium
    C) Marquette Stadium
    D) City Stadium

48) How many Green Bay receivers had 50 or more catches in the 2010 regular season?

    A) 1
    B) 2
    C) 3
    D) 5

49) When was the last time Green Bay led the NFL in rushing defense?

    A) 1996
    B) 2000
    C) 2005
    D) 2009

50) What is the Green Bay record for most consecutive playoff losses?

    A) 2
    B) 4
    C) 5
    D) 7

Packerology Trivia Challenge

Super Bowl XLV between Green Bay and Pittsburgh was the first since Super Bowl II without cheerleaders for either side. The teams join just four others without official cheerleaders – the Chicago Bears, Detroit Lions, Cleveland Browns and New York Giants. Since 1988, cheerleaders from either the University of Wisconsin-Green Bay or St. Norbert College perform at Packer home games. Even though cheerleaders from these colleges attended the previous two Packer Super Bowl appearances, they did not make the trip for the win against the Steelers. Pittsburgh has not had official cheerleaders since the 1970s. Even without the sideline entertainment, the play of the Steelers in the second quarter of Super Bowl XLV provided plenty of excitement for Packer fans. And even though no "official" cheerleaders graced the sidelines, the game had an average audience of 111 million viewers, making it the most watched telecast in U.S. history.

1) B – 2 (The Packers lost 27-28 to the Cowboys in the 1995 NFC Championship game and 20-23 to the Giants in 2007.)

2) B – $250 (The Packers had their franchise forfeited in 1921 after using college players in a game against Chicago. Lambeau chipped in $50 and got the rest from a friend.)

3) A – 1929 (The Packers went 12-0-1 en route to their first NFL Championship.)

4) D – Vince Lombardi (98 wins from 1959-67)

5) C – 37 (The Packers beat the Giants 37-0 in the 1961 NFL Championship game.)

6) A – James Lofton (Lofton gained 9,656 yards in nine seasons with the Packers [1978-86].)

7) D – Bart Starr (The highest single game touchdown total for Starr was four. Favre had three five-touchdown games, Dickey had two, Horn had one, and Cecil Isbell also had one.)

8) A – 0 (Will Blackmon returned two punts for touchdowns in 2008, the last time a Packer scored on a punt or kickoff return.)

9) C – 8 (Don Chandler completed all eight attempts against Atlanta on Oct. 23, 1966.)

10) C – 1950s (The highest win total for GB in the '50s was 7-5 in 1959. The Packers won 10 or more games/season 18 times since joining the NFL.)

11) A – True (Green Bay is 21-35 [.600] for two-point conversions, with all successful conversions occurring on pass plays.)

12) C – 5 (The Packers went 2-3 in games when Rodgers passed for 300 or more yards.)

13) D – 10 (Mike Douglass led the team in 1984, Tim Harris from 1986-90, Tony Bennett from 1991-92 and Clay Matthews from 2009-10.)

14) B – Irv Comp (He pulled down 10 interceptions in 10 games in 1943, his rookie season.)

15) B – Vince Lombardi (.758 winning percentage [98-30-4])

16) C – 628 yards (The Packers rushed for 294 yards and passed for 334 against the Eagles in 1962.)

17) A – A.J. Hawk (He recorded 155 tackles during his rookie season in 2006.)

18) C – 9 (The Packers lost nine straight games spanning the 1948-49 seasons. Green Bay was outscored by an average of 22.8 points during that streak.)

19) C – 1973 (Jerry Tagge led the Packers with 720 yards passing.)

20) B – Sterling Sharpe (Sharpe led the team in 1994 with 108 points off 18 touchdowns.)

21) D – .641 (The Packers have an all-time record of 388-214-16 at home.)

22) A – Yes (The official cheerleading group was dissolved after the 1988 season. Cheerleaders from local colleges currently perform at home games.)

23) D – Reggie White (White's number was retired in 2005 after his death in 2004. White played for the Packers from 1993-98.)

24) C – 2003 (The Packer offense gained 2,558 rushing yards on 507 carries and scored 18 rushing TDs.)

25) A – True (Favre had 721 career playoff pass attempts in 22 games and Starr had 213 pass attempts in 10 games.)

26) D – Miami Dolphins (The Packers played overtime games against the Dolphins and the Redskins in 2010, losing both.)

27) D – Chester Marcol (He won the award in 1972 after leading the NFL in scoring [128 points]. The award was given from 1970-96 and John Brockington was the only other Packer recipient [1971].)

28) B – 5 (Terdell Middleton in 1978, Gerry Ellis in 1980, Brent Fullwood in 1988, Sterling Sharpe in 1994, and Ahman Green in 2003)

29) B – 1996 (The Packers beat the Vikings 38-10 to get their 1,000th league win.)

30) A – .380 (One-year coaches had a combined record of 17-28-1 with the Packers.)

31) A – 1 (Brandon Jackson [115 yards, Week 5])

32) D – 15 years (The Packers failed to make the playoffs from 1945-59. The 1950s is the only decade that Green Bay never had a playoff appearance.)

33) B – San Diego Chargers (The Packers have an all-time record of 8-1 against San Diego.)

34) A – Touchdown Pass (Max McGee pulled in a 37-yard pass from Bart Starr to put the Packers up 7-0. This was his first of two touchdowns on the day.)

35) B – No (The lowest single-season rushing-yard total as a team for the Packers was 1,081 yards in 1982.)

36) C – 255 (His first start was Sept. 27, 1992, against Minnesota and he did not miss another game as a Packer.)

37) D – Derek Sherrod (Green Bay drafted Sherrod [OT] out of Mississippi St. with the 32nd pick overall.)

38) D – Tobin Rote (He led the team in passing and rushing in 1952 and 1956.)

39) C – Bart Starr (Starr punched it in from the one yard line with 13 seconds left in the game.)

40) A – 1998 (Darick Holmes led the Packers with 386 rushing yards on 93 carries, scoring just one rushing touchdown.)

41) B – 1997 (The Packers followed an undefeated preseason with a 13-3 regular-season record and Super Bowl win.)

42) D – 53 (Green Bay beat Atlanta 56-3 in 1966.)

43) A – Texas (Coach Dan Devine implemented spring practice his first season with the Packers in 1971. The team practiced at the University of Texas.)

44) B – Gene Ronzani (Gene coached the Packers to an overall record of 14-31-1 [.354] from 1950-53.)

45) C – Jordy Nelson (The Packers never trailed after gaining a 7-0 lead following Nelson's 29-yard reception from Aaron Rodgers in the first quarter.)

46) A – Yes (His Packers beat the Oakland Raiders 33-14 in Super Bowl II.)

47) D – City Stadium (Built in 1925, seating capacity reached just over 25,000.)

48) C – 3 (Greg Jennings [76], Donald Driver [51] and James Jones [50])

49) D – 2009 (This was just the second time leading the league in rushing defense since 1967.)

50) A – 2 (The Packers have lost two straight playoff games on four occasions.)

Note: All answers valid as of the end of the 2010 season, unless otherwise indicated in the question itself.

1) When was the last time a Packers game resulted in a tie?

Answers begin on page 75

   A)   1987
   B)   1991
   C)   1995
   D)   2000

2) Which opponent handed Green Bay its only home loss in 2010?

   A)   Detroit Lions
   B)   Miami Dolphins
   C)   New England Patriots
   D)   Chicago Bears

3) How many Packers have had their numbers retired?

   A)   2
   B)   4
   C)   5
   D)   7

4) Has a Packer running back ever had five rushing touchdowns in a single game?

   A)   Yes
   B)   No

5) Which Packer kicked the most career game-winning/game-saving field goals?

    A) Jan Stenerud
    B) Al Del Greco
    C) Ryan Longwell
    D) Chris Jacke

6) Who was the last Packer head coach to win his first regular-season NFL game?

    A) Mike McCarthy
    B) Mike Sherman
    C) Ray Rhodes
    D) Mike Holmgren

7) What is the Green Bay record for most consecutive years appearing in the playoffs?

    A) 4
    B) 6
    C) 7
    D) 9

8) How many Green Bay coaches are in the Pro Football Hall of Fame?

    A) 1
    B) 2
    C) 4
    D) 5

9) Against which AFC team does Green Bay have the worst all-time winning percentage (min. 3 games)?

 A) Buffalo Bills
 B) Indianapolis Colts
 C) Pittsburgh Steelers
 D) Miami Dolphins

10) Did Earl Lambeau have a winning record when coaching against the Packers?

 A) Yes
 B) No

11) Which of the following players was not named a Consensus All-Pro in 1998?

 A) Brett Favre
 B) Reggie White
 C) LeRoy Butler
 D) Antonio Freeman

12) When was the last time the Packers had two players gain over 100 yards rushing in the same game?

 A) 1997
 B) 2001
 C) 2005
 D) 2008

13) In which of the following categories did the Green Bay defense lead the NFC in 2010?

   A) Third down percentage
   B) Fewest successful fourth down attempts
   C) Fewest rushing yards allowed on first down
   D) Fewest yards after catch allowed

14) Who holds the Green Bay single season rushing record?

   A) Dorsey Levins
   B) Ahman Green
   C) Edgar Bennett
   D) Jim Taylor

15) When was the last time the Packers were shut out?

   A) 1998
   B) 2001
   C) 2004
   D) 2006

16) Brett Favre passed for more than 3,000 yards every season with Green Bay.

   A) True
   B) False

17) What year did a black quarterback first play for the Packers?

    A) 1948
    B) 1955
    C) 1961
    D) 1970

18) When was the last time the Packers had two receivers with over 1,000 yards receiving in the same season?

    A) 2000
    B) 2004
    C) 2006
    D) 2009

19) Who holds the Green Bay records for rushing touchdowns in a game, season and career?

    A) Jim Brockington
    B) Paul Hornung
    C) Jim Taylor
    D) Ahman Green

20) Which Green Bay quarterback holds the record for the highest passer rating in a single season?

    A) Brett Favre
    B) Lynn Dickey
    C) Randy Wright
    D) Bart Starr

21) How many head coaches have the Packers had in their history?

    A) 14
    B) 17
    C) 21
    D) 23

22) What is Green Bay's largest margin of victory over Chicago?

    A) 30
    B) 37
    C) 43
    D) 49

23) Which head coach has the second best winning percentage at Green Bay (min. 3 seasons)?

    A) Dan Devine
    B) Mike Sherman
    C) Mike Holmgren
    D) Curly Lambeau

24) Has Green Bay played every NFL team at least once?

    A) Yes
    B) No

25) Which Packer player won the Ed Block Courage Award in 2010?

    A) A.J. Hawk
    B) Brett Swain
    C) Ryan Grant
    D) Charles Woodson

26) Green Bay has an all-time winning record against every NFC North opponent.

    A) True
    B) False

27) What year was the City of Green Bay first referred to as "Titletown"?

    A) 1936
    B) 1949
    C) 1961
    D) 1970

28) Who was the last Packer to lead the NFL in yards per kickoff return?

    A) Desmond Howard
    B) Allen Rossum
    C) Robert Brooks
    D) Najeh Davenport

29) In which decade did Green Bay have its worst winning percentage?

A) 1920s
B) 1940s
C) 1950s
D) 1970s

30) The Packers were penalized for over 1,000 yards in 2010.

A) True
B) False

31) When was the last time the Packers rushed for over 300 yards as a team?

A) 1953
B) 1962
C) 1988
D) 1997

32) Who is the only Super Bowl opponent to have had a halftime lead against the Packers?

A) Kanas City Chiefs
B) Oakland Raiders
C) New England Patriots
D) Denver Broncos

33) When was the last time the Packers gave up a safety?

    A) 1994
    B) 2001
    C) 2005
    D) 2009

34) What is the worst defeat Green Bay has suffered in a
    playoff game?

    A) 26 points
    B) 29 points
    C) 32 points
    D) 35 points

35) What is the Green Bay record for consecutive regular
    season wins?

    A) 8
    B) 9
    C) 11
    D) 13

36) Since 1970, has Green Bay ever led the league in
    rushing offense, passing offense or total offense?

    A) Yes
    B) No

37) How many stripes are on the sleeves of the Packers jersey?

    A) 2
    B) 3
    C) 5
    D) 7

38) Who led Green Bay in interceptions in 2010?

    A) Sam Shields
    B) Charles Woodson
    C) Tramon Williams
    D) Nick Collins

39) Who holds the Green Bay record for most consecutive seasons leading the team in total tackles?

    A) Brian Noble
    B) Reggie White
    C) Rich Wingo
    D) Nick Barnett

40) Do the Packers have a regular season winning record against the previous year's Super Bowl Champion?

    A) Yes
    B) No

41) How big is the largest crowd to ever watch a Packers football game at Lambeau Field?

    A) 70,677
    B) 72,740
    C) 74,984
    D) 76,019

42) What year did the Packers first play the "Shrine Game"?

    A) 1936
    B) 1943
    C) 1950
    D) 1959

43) Which of the following Packer quarterbacks never had a 400-yard passing game?

    A) Bart Starr
    B) Don Horn
    C) Brett Favre
    D) Lynn Dickey

44) What was the best winning percentage of a Green Bay head coach who only lasted one season?

    A) .500
    B) .634
    C) .756
    D) .825

45) Who was the last opponent Green Bay shut out?

    A)   Seattle Seahawks
    B)   Minnesota Vikings
    C)   Chicago Bears
    D)   New York Jets

46) Who holds the Green Bay record for most points scored in a single season?

    A)   Paul Hornung
    B)   Jim Taylor
    C)   Ahman Green
    D)   James Lofton

47) What are the most touchdown passes by Brett Favre against a single team in his career?

    A)   41
    B)   48
    C)   54
    D)   61

48) What is the Green Bay record for most consecutive wins at home?

    A)   18
    B)   20
    C)   22
    D)   25

49) Who holds the Green Bay single-game rushing-record in the playoffs?

   A) Edgar Bennett
   B) Ahman Green
   C) Ryan Grant
   D) Jim Taylor

50) What is the color of the letters of the stadium sign at Lambeau Field?

   A) White
   B) Yellow
   C) Green
   D) Black

In 1958 Green Bay finished with just one win under head coach Ray McLean, who resigned at the end of the season. His replacement, Vince Lombardi, rose to legendary status. It would all start, however, on Sept. 27, 1959, in Green Bay's first game of the season - against the rival Chicago Bears. From 1940-58, the Packers had a record of 8-27-2 (.243) against the Bears. Lombardi's leadership would help change the tide in this rivalry. The game on Sept. 27 started as most other games between these teams for the previous 20 years, with Chicago jumping out to an early lead. But Paul Hornung's point after touchdown following Jim Taylor's rushing touchdown in the fourth quarter, gave Green Bay the lead for good. The win ended a seven-game losing streak and helped the team to a 7-5 record for the season, its first winning season since 1947. Lombardi, who never had a losing season with the Packers, finished his career with a 12-6 record against the Bears.

1) A – 1987 (Green Bay tied Denver 17-17 in Milwaukee.)

2) B – Miami Dolphins (The Packers suffered a 20-23 overtime loss to the Dolphins in Week 6.)

3) C – 5 (Tony Canadeo [#3], Don Hutson [#14], Bart Starr [#15], Ray Nitschke [#66] and Reggie White [#92])

4) B – No (Packer running backs have rushed for four touchdowns in a single game on five occasions, most recently Dorsey Levins in 2000.)

5) C – Ryan Longwell (Longwell kicked 11 game-winning/game-saving field goals from 1998-05.)

6) C – Ray Rhodes (In 1999 Green Bay beat the Raiders in Rhodes' first official game. Packer head coaches are 5-9 in their official NFL head coaching debuts.)

7) B – 6 (Playoff appearances every year from 1994-99)

8) B – 2 (Curly Lambeau 1963 and Vince Lombardi 1971)

9) D – Miami Dolphins (Green Bay has an all-time record of 3-10 against Miami for a .231 winning percentage.)

10) B – No (After coaching the Packers, Lambeau coached the Cardinals from 1950-51 and the Redskins from 1952-53. His only matchup with the Packers was a 20-35 loss in 1952 as coach of the Redskins.)

11) A – Brett Favre (Although Favre was a Consensus All-Pro from 1995-97, he was not one of the three Packers named in 1998.)

12) D – 2008 (Ryan Grant and DeShawn Wynn each rushed for 106 yards vs. Detroit on Dec. 28. It was the fifth time in Green Bay history that two players rushed for 100+ yards in the same game.)

13) C – Fewest rushing yards allowed on first down (The Packer defense allowed 82 rushing yards on first down, best in the NFC, fourth best in the NFL.)

14) B – Ahman Green (Green gained 1,883 yards on 355 carries in 2003.)

15) D – 2006 (Green Bay lost 0-35 at home to the Patriots.)

16) A – True (The lowest season total for Favre was 3,227 yards in 1992 after starting only 13 games.)

17) B – 1955 (Charles Brackins made the team as the only black quarterback in the league that year. He only threw two passes against Cleveland before being released. It was not until 1968 that another black quarterback played in the NFL.)

18) D – 2009 (This was the second consecutive year Donald Driver and Greg Jennings each surpassed the 1,000+ yard receiving mark and the fifth time in Packer history that two players accomplished the feat in one season.)

19) C – Jim Taylor (Taylor recorded 81 touchdowns from 1958-66, 19 touchdowns in 1962, and four touchdowns in a game on three occasions [also accomplished once by Dorsey Levins and Terdell Middleton].)

20) D – Bart Starr (He set the team record in 1966 with a rating of 105.0. He finished the season with 156 completions on 251 attempts [.622], 14 touchdowns, 3 interceptions, and 2,257 yards.)

21) A – 14 (Starting with Curly Lambeau to Mike McCarthy)

22) D – 49 (The Packers shut out the Bears 49-0 in 1962.)

23) C – Mike Holmgren (Holmgren went 75-32 from 1992-98 for a .670 winning percentage.)

24) A – Yes (Green Bay has played the Houston Texans the least amount of times. The teams have met just twice, with each team winning once.)

25) D – Charles Woodson (This award is given to a player from each team that exemplifies and displays courage. The team voted to give this award to Woodson for his on-the-field leadership.)

26) B – False (Green Bay's all-time record against: Chicago is 83-91-6 [.478]; Detroit 89-65-7 [.575]; and Minnesota 51-47-1 [.575].)

27) C – 1961 (Green Bay Press-Gazette employee Jack Yuenger first referred to Green Bay as "Titletown" following the Packers' 1961 NFL Championship win against the Giants.)

28) D – Najeh Davenport (He led the league in 2003 with a 31.6 yard return average.)

29) C – 1950s (The Packers went 39-79-2 for a .333 winning percentage.)

30) B – False (The Packers were penalized 78 times for 617 yards.)

31) A – 1953 (The Packers gained 303 yards against the Colts for only their second win of the season. As a team, Green Bay has only rushed for 300+ yards in a game on four occasions [1946, 301 yards; 1947, 366 yards; and 1950, 312 yards].)

32) D – Denver Broncos (Denver led 17-14 at halftime in Super Bowl XXXII before winning 31-24.)

33) D – 2009 (Ryan Grant was tackled in the end zone by Louis Delmas of the Lions in Week 12.)

34) B – 29 points (The Packers lost 14-33 to the Bears in the 1941 Western Divisional Playoffs.)

35) C – 11 (Green Bay has won 11 straight seasons on two occasions, from 1928-29 and again from 1961-62.)

36) B – No (The highest ranking for total offense and passing offense is No. 2 on two occasions in the same year, 1983 and 2007. Highest ranking for rushing offense is No. 3 in 2003.)

37) B – 3 (Two yellow and one white stripe. The number of stripes has varied throughout the years, most recently with three stripes since 1997.)

38) C – Tramon Williams (Williams led the team with six interceptions.)

39) D – Nick Barnett (He led them three consecutive years: 134 tackles in 2003, 162 in 2004 and 194 in 2005.)

40) B – No (The Packers are 6-13 [.316] all-time against Super Bowl winners from the previous year.)

41) B – 72,740 (The 2007 NFC Championship between the Packers and the Giants drew the largest crowd ever at Lambeau Field.)

42) C – 1950 (Every year the team donates a portion of the proceeds from this game to the Shriners' Hospital and has raised over $3.1 million dollars since 1950.)

43) A – Bart Starr (Dickey passed for 418 yards against the Bucs in 1980, Horn passed for 410 yards against the Cardinals in 1969 and Favre passed for 402 yards against the Bears in 1993.)

44) A – .500 (In 1999 Ray Rhodes finished 8-8, his only season with the Packers.)

45) D – New York Jets (Green Bay beat the Jets 9-0 in Week 8 of 2010.)

46) A – Paul Hornung (The "Golden Boy" scored 176 points in 1960 off 15 touchdowns, 41 PATs, and 15 field goals. This was the league record until broken by LaDainian Tomlinson in 2006.)

47) C – 54 (Favre threw 54 career touchdown passes against both Detroit and Minnesota.)

48) D – 25 (Green Bay won 25 straight home games from 1995-98.)

49) C – Ryan Grant (Grant stormed over the Seahawks for 201 yards on 27 carries for three touchdowns in the 2007 Divisional Playoffs.)

50) A – White (Located at the north end of the stadium, the green sign has a white "G" logo with the words "Lambeau Field" below.)

Note: All answers valid as of the end of the 2010 season, unless otherwise indicated in the question itself.

1) Which player has caught the most touchdown passes thrown by Brett Favre?

Answers begin on page 83

A)   Sterling Sharpe
B)   Donald Driver
C)   Robert Brooks
D)   Antonio Freeman

2) What is the longest winning streak for the Packers in the Green Bay-Chicago series?

A)   7
B)   8
C)   10
D)   12

3) How many Packers have played in five or more Pro Bowls?

A)   4
B)   6
C)   8
D)   11

4) Green Bay has the best playoff winning percentage in the NFL.

A)   True
B)   False

5) Which team ended up with the 17th pick in the first round that Green Bay traded to get Brett Favre?

   A) Dallas Cowboys
   B) Atlanta Falcons
   C) Minnesota Vikings
   D) Miami Dolphins

6) Against which NFL Division does Green Bay have the best all-time winning percentage?

   A) AFC North
   B) NFC East
   C) AFC West
   D) NFC South

7) What year did the Packers finish the season with only one win?

   A) 1937
   B) 1949
   C) 1958
   D) 1971

8) Who is the only Packer to be named Pro Bowl MVP?

   A) James Lofton
   B) Brett Favre
   C) Reggie White
   D) John Jefferson

9) How many regular-season touchdown drives of 80 yards or more did the Packers have in 2007?

    A) 9
    B) 11
    C) 13
    D) 16

10) What are the most points scored by Green Bay in a single game?

    A) 54
    B) 57
    C) 62
    D) 65

1) D – Antonio Freeman (57 touchdown receptions)
2) C – 10 (Green Bay won every meeting from 1994-98.)
3) D – 11 (Jim Taylor [5], Herb Adderley [5], Willie Davis [5], Gale Gillingham [5], Sterling Sharpe [5], Reggie White [6], Jim Ringo [7], James Lofton [7], Brett Favre [8], Willie Wood [8] and Forrest Gregg [9])
4) A – True (The Packers have a playoff record of 29-16 for a .644 winning percentage.)
5) A – Dallas Cowboys (The Cowboys drafted cornerback Kevin Smith, who played from 1992-99.)
6) D – NFC South (61-44-1, .580 winning percentage)
7) C – 1958 (Green Bay finished the season 1-10-1 [.091].)
8) D – John Jefferson (This Green Bay wide receiver was tied with quarterback Dan Fouts for MVP in 1982.)
9) A – 9 (Once against Washington, Miami, Minnesota, New England and the Giants and two times against Dallas and Atlanta.)
10) B – 57 (The Packers beat the Lions 57-21 on Oct. 7, 1945.)

Note: All answers valid as of the end of the 2010 season, unless otherwise indicated in the question itself.

Player / Team Score Sheet

Name:_____

First Quarter				Second Quarter				Third Quarter				Fourth Quarter				Overtime Bonus	
1		26		1		26		1		26		1		26		1	
2		27		2		27		2		27		2		27		2	
3		28		3		28		3		28		3		28		3	
4		29		4		29		4		29		4		29		4	
5		30		5		30		5		30		5		30		5	
6		31		6		31		6		31		6		31		6	
7		32		7		32		7		32		7		32		7	
8		33		8		33		8		33		8		33		8	
9		34		9		34		9		34		9		34		9	
10		35		10		35		10		35		10		35		10	
11		36		11		36		11		36		11		36			
12		37		12		37		12		37		12		37			
13		38		13		38		13		38		13		38			
14		39		14		39		14		39		14		39			
15		40		15		40		15		40		15		40			
16		41		16		41		16		41		16		41			
17		42		17		42		17		42		17		42			
18		43		18		43		18		43		18		43			
19		44		19		44		19		44		19		44			
20		45		20		45		20		45		20		45			
21		46		21		46		21		46		21		46			
22		47		22		47		22		47		22		47			
23		48		23		48		23		48		23		48			
24		49		24		49		24		49		24		49			
25		50		25		50		25		50		25		50			

___ x 1 =___   ___ x 2 =___   ___ x 3 =___   ___ x 4 =___   ___ x 4 =___

Multiply total number correct by point value/quarter to calculate totals for each quarter.

Add total of all quarters below.

Total Points:_____

Thank you for playing *Packerology Trivia Challenge*.

**Additional score sheets are available at:
www.TriviaGameBooks.com**

Player / Team Score Sheet

Name:_____

First Quarter		Second Quarter		Third Quarter		Fourth Quarter		Overtime Bonus	
1	26	1	26	1	26	1	26	1	
2	27	2	27	2	27	2	27	2	
3	28	3	28	3	28	3	28	3	
4	29	4	29	4	29	4	29	4	
5	30	5	30	5	30	5	30	5	
6	31	6	31	6	31	6	31	6	
7	32	7	32	7	32	7	32	7	
8	33	8	33	8	33	8	33	8	
9	34	9	34	9	34	9	34	9	
10	35	10	35	10	35	10	35	10	
11	36	11	36	11	36	11	36		
12	37	12	37	12	37	12	37		
13	38	13	38	13	38	13	38		
14	39	14	39	14	39	14	39		
15	40	15	40	15	40	15	40		
16	41	16	41	16	41	16	41		
17	42	17	42	17	42	17	42		
18	43	18	43	18	43	18	43		
19	44	19	44	19	44	19	44		
20	45	20	45	20	45	20	45		
21	46	21	46	21	46	21	46		
22	47	22	47	22	47	22	47		
23	48	23	48	23	48	23	48		
24	49	24	49	24	49	24	49		
25	50	25	50	25	50	25	50		
___ x 1 =___		___ x 2 =___		___ x 3 =___		___ x 4 =___		___ x 4 =___	

Multiply total number correct by point value/quarter to calculate totals for each quarter.

Add total of all quarters below.

Total Points:_____

Thank you for playing *Packerology Trivia Challenge*.

Additional score sheets are available at:
www.TriviaGameBooks.com